PUSHKIN PRESS — THE LONDON LIBRARY

The London Library is the world's largest independent library. Founded in 1841 by Thomas Carlyle (in reaction to the "museum headache" brought on by the crowds in the British Museum Reading Room), it has become a haven for readers, writers and all who draw strength, solace or inspiration from the presence of books. Some of the most illustrious figures of the last two centuries have written, thought and walked there: George Eliot, Charles Dickens, E.M. Forster, Virginia Woolf and many more were members.

And over time, some of these celebrated members have shared—with each other, or with an interested public—their views on the delights, challenges and joys of reading, writing and living with books.

The books in "Found on the Shelves" have been chosen to give a fascinating insight into the treasures that can be found while browsing in The London Library. Now celebrating its 175th anniversary, with over seventeen miles of shelving and more than a million books, The London Library has become an unrivalled archive of the modes, manners and thoughts of each generation which has helped to form it.

From essays on dieting in the 1860s to instructions for gentlewomen on trout-fishing, from advice on the ill health caused by the "modern" craze of bicycling to travelogues from Norway, they are as readable and relevant today as they were more than a century ago.

ON READING, WRITING AND LIVING WITH BOOKS

The London Library

Pushkin Press

Pushkin Press
71–75 Shelton Street,
London WC2H 9JQ

Virginia Woolf, "How Should One Read a Book?" from *The Common
Reader: Second Series*. London: Leonard & Virginia Woolf at The
Hogarth Press, 1932

Charles Dickens, Letter to Wilkie Collins, 20 December 1852 from *The
Letters of Charles Dickens, 1833 to 1870*, edited by his Sister-in Law
and his Eldest Daughter. London: Macmillan and Co., 1893

Charles Dickens, Letter to George Eliot, 18 January 1858 from *George
Eliot's Life as Related in her Letters and Journals*, arranged and edited
by her husband J.W. Cross, v2. Edinburgh: William Blackwood and
Sons, 1885

George Eliot, "Authorship" from *Essays and Leaves from a Notebook*,
2nd ed. Edinburgh: William Blackwood and Sons, 1884

Leigh Hunt, "My Books" from *The World of Books, and Other Essays*.
London: Gay and Bird, 1899

E.M. Forster, "The London Library" from *Two Cheers for Democracy*.
London: Edward Arnold & Co., 1951. United States copyright 1939 by
E.M. Forster. Copyright © Renewed 1967 by E.M. Forster. Reprinted
by permission of Houghton Mifflin Harcourt Publishing Company. All
rights reserved. United Kingdom © The Provost and Scholars of King's
College, Cambridge and The Society of Authors as the E.M. Forster
Estate

First published by Pushkin Press in 2016

9 8 7 6 5 4 3 2

ISBN 978 1 782272 51 9

Set in Goudy Modern by Tetragon, London

Printed by CPI Group (UK) Ltd, Croydon, CR0 4YY

www.pushkinpress.com

HOW SHOULD ONE READ A BOOK?

Published in 1932

BY VIRGINIA WOOLF

VIRGINIA WOOLF (1882–1941) was the daughter of Leslie Stephen, who was President of The London Library from 1892 until his death in 1904. During his lifetime, Virginia had access to the collections of the Library, and she joined in her own right just four days after his death, giving her occupation as "Spinster". She was one of the greatest novelists and essayists of the twentieth century.

In the first place, I want to emphasise the note of interrogation at the end of my title. Even if I could answer the question for myself, the answer would apply only to me and not to you. The only advice, indeed, that one person can give another about reading is to take no advice, to follow your own instincts, to use your own reason, to come to your own conclusions. If this is agreed between us, then I feel at liberty to put forward a few ideas and suggestions because you will not allow them to fetter that independence which is the most important quality that a reader can possess. After all, what laws can be laid down about books? The battle of Waterloo was certainly fought on a certain day; but is *Hamlet* a better play than *Lear*? Nobody can say. Each must decide that question for himself. To admit authorities, however heavily furred and gowned, into our libraries and let them tell us how to read, what to read, what value to place upon what we read, is to destroy the spirit of freedom which is the breath of those sanctuaries. Everywhere else we may be bound by laws and conventions—there we have none.

But to enjoy freedom, if the platitude is pardonable, we have of course to control ourselves. We must not squander our powers, helplessly and ignorantly, squirting half the house in order to water a single rose-bush; we must train them, exactly and powerfully, here on the very spot. This, it may be, is one of the first difficulties that faces us in a library. What is "the very spot"? There may well seem to be nothing but a conglomeration and huddle of confusion. Poems and novels, histories and memoirs, dictionaries and blue-books; books written in all languages by men and women of all tempers, races, and ages jostle each other on the shelf. And outside the donkey brays, the women gossip at the pump, the colts gallop across the fields. Where are we to begin? How are we to bring order into this multitudinous chaos and so get the deepest and widest pleasure from what we read?

It is simple enough to say that since books have classes—fiction, biography, poetry—we should separate them and take from each what it is right that each should give us. Yet few people ask from books what books can give us. Most commonly we come to books with blurred and divided minds, asking of fiction that it shall be true, of poetry that it shall be false, of biography that it shall be flattering, of history that it shall enforce our own prejudices. If we could banish all such preconceptions when we read, that would be an admirable beginning. Do not dictate to your author; try to become him. Be his fellow-worker and accomplice. If you hang back, and reserve and criticise at first, you are preventing yourself from getting the fullest possible value from what you read. But if you open your mind as widely as possible, then signs and hints of almost imperceptible fineness, from the twist and turn of the first sentences, will bring you into the presence of a human being unlike any other. Steep yourself in this, acquaint yourself with this, and soon you will find that your author is giving you, or attempting to give you, something far more definite. The thirty-two chapters of a novel—if we consider how to read a novel first—are an attempt to make something as formed and controlled as a building: but words are more impalpable than bricks; reading is a longer and more complicated process than seeing. Perhaps the quickest way to understand the elements of what a novelist is doing is not to read, but to write; to make your own experiment with the dangers and difficulties of words. Recall, then, some event that has left a distinct impression on you—how at the corner of the street, perhaps, you passed two people talking. A tree shook; an electric light danced; the tone of the talk was comic, but also tragic; a whole vision, an entire conception, seemed contained in that moment.

But when you attempt to reconstruct it in words, you will find that it breaks into a thousand conflicting impressions. Some must be subdued; others emphasised; in the process you will lose, probably, all grasp upon the emotion itself. Then turn from your blurred and littered pages to the opening pages of some great novelist—Defoe, Jane Austen, Hardy. Now you will be better able to appreciate their mastery. It is not merely that we are in the presence of a different person— Defoe, Jane Austen, or Thomas Hardy—but that we are living in a different world. Here, in *Robinson Crusoe*, we are trudging a plain high road; one thing happens after another; the fact and the order of the fact is enough. But if the open air and adventure mean everything to Defoe they mean nothing to Jane Austen. Hers is the drawing-room, and people talking, and by the many mirrors of their talk revealing their characters. And if, when we have accustomed ourselves to the drawing-room and its reflections, we turn to Hardy, we are once more spun round. The moors are round us and the stars are above our heads. The other side of the mind is now exposed—the dark side that comes uppermost in solitude, not the light side that shows in company. Our relations are not towards people, but towards Nature and destiny. Yet different as these worlds are, each is consistent with itself. The maker of each is careful to observe the laws of his own perspective, and however great a strain they may put upon us they will never confuse us, as lesser writers so frequently do, by introducing two different kinds of reality into the same book. Thus to go from one great novelist to another—from

Jane Austen to Hardy, from Peacock to Trollope, from Scott to Meredith—is to be wrenched and uprooted; to be thrown this way and then that. To read a novel is a difficult and complex art. You must be capable not only of great fineness of perception, but of great boldness of imagination if you are going to make use of all that the novelist—the great artist—gives you.

But a glance at the heterogeneous company on the shelf will show you that writers are very seldom "great artists"; far more often a book makes no claim to be a work of art at all. These biographies and autobiographies, for example, lives of great men, of men long dead and forgotten, that stand cheek by jowl with the novels and poems, are we to refuse to read them because they are not "art"? Or shall we read them, but read them in a different way, with a different aim? Shall we read them in the first place to satisfy that curiosity which possesses us sometimes when in the evening we linger in front of a house where the lights are lit and the blinds not yet drawn, and each floor of the house shows us a different section of human life in being? Then we are consumed with curiosity about the lives of these people—the servants gossiping, the gentlemen dining, the girl dressing for a party, the old woman at the window with her knitting. Who are they, what are they, what are their names, their occupations, their thoughts, and adventures?

Biographies and memoirs answer such questions, light up innumerable such houses; they show us people going about their daily affairs, toiling, failing, succeeding, eating, hating, loving, until they die. And sometimes as we watch, the house fades and the iron railings vanish and we are out at sea; we are hunting, sailing, fighting; we are among savages and soldiers; we are taking part in great campaigns. Or if we like to stay here in England, in London, still the scene changes; the street narrows; the house becomes small, cramped, diamond-paned, and malodorous. We see a poet, Donne, driven from such a house because the walls were so thin that when the children cried their voices cut through them. We can follow him, through the paths that lie in the pages of books, to Twickenham; to Lady Bedford's Park, a famous meeting-ground for nobles and poets; and then turn our steps to Wilton, the great house under the downs, and hear Sidney read the *Arcadia* to his sister; and ramble among the very marshes and see the very herons that figure in that famous romance; and then again travel north with that other Lady Pembroke, Anne Clifford, to her wild moors, or plunge into the city and control our merriment at the sight of Gabriel Harvey in his black velvet suit arguing about poetry with Spenser. Nothing is more fascinating than to grope and stumble in the alternate darkness and splendour of Elizabethan London. But there is no staying there. The Temples and the Swifts, the Harleys and the St. Johns beckon us on; hour upon hour can be spent disentangling their quarrels and deciphering their characters; and when we tire of them we can stroll on, past a lady in black wearing diamonds, to Samuel Johnson and Goldsmith and Garrick; or cross the channel, if we like, and meet Voltaire and Diderot, Madame du Deffand; and so back to England and Twickenham—how certain places repeat themselves and certain names!— where Lady Bedford had her Park once and Pope lived later, to Walpole's home at Strawberry Hill.

But Walpole introduces us to such a swarm of new acquaintances, there are so many houses to visit and bells to ring that we may well hesitate for a moment, on the Miss Berrys' doorstep, for example, when behold, up comes Thackeray; he is the friend of the woman whom Walpole loved; so that merely by going from friend to friend, from garden to garden, from house to house, we have passed from one end of English literature to another and wake to find ourselves here again in the present, if we can so differentiate this moment from all that have gone before. This, then, is one of the ways in which we can read these lives and letters; we can make them light up the many windows of the past; we can watch the famous dead in their familiar habits and fancy sometimes that we are very close and can surprise their secrets, and sometimes we may pull out a play or a poem that they have written and see whether it reads differently in the presence of the author. But this again rouses other questions. How far, we must ask ourselves, is a book influenced by its writer's life—how far is it safe to let the man interpret the writer? How far shall we resist or give way to the sympathies and antipathies that the man himself rouses in us—so sensitive are words, so receptive of the character of the author? These are questions that press upon us when we read lives and letters, and we must answer them for ourselves, for nothing can be more fatal than to be guided by the preferences of others in a matter so personal.

But also we can read such books with another aim, not to throw light on literature, not to become familiar with famous people, but to refresh and exercise our own creative powers. Is there not an open window on the right hand of the bookcase? How delightful to stop reading and look out! How stimulating the scene is, in its unconsciousness, its irrelevance, its perpetual movement—the colts galloping round the field, the woman filling her pail at the well, the donkey throwing back his head and emitting his long, acrid moan. The greater part of any library is nothing but the record of such fleeting moments in the lives of men, women, and donkeys. Every literature, as it grows old, has its rubbish-heap, its record of vanished moments and forgotten lives told in faltering and feeble accents that have perished. But if you give yourself up to the delight of rubbish-reading you will be surprised, indeed you will be overcome, by the relics of human life that have been cast out to moulder. It may be one letter—but what a vision it gives! It may be a few sentences—but what vistas they suggest! Sometimes a whole story will come together with such beautiful humour and pathos and completeness that it seems as if a great novelist had been at work, yet it is only an old actor, Tate Wilkinson, remembering the strange story of Captain Jones; it is only a young subaltern serving under Arthur Wellesley and falling in love with a pretty girl at Lisbon; it is only Maria Allen letting fall her sewing in the empty drawing-room and sighing how she wishes she had taken Dr. Burney's good advice and had never eloped with her Rishy. None of this has any value; it is negligible in the extreme; yet how absorbing it is now and again to go through the rubbish-heaps and find rings and scissors and broken noses buried in the huge past and try to piece them together while the colt gallops round the field, the woman fills her pail at the well, and the donkey brays.

But we tire of rubbish-reading in the long run. We tire of searching for what is needed to complete the half-truth which is all that the Wilkinsons, the Bunburys, and the Maria Allens are able to offer us. They had not the artist's power of mastering and eliminating; they could not tell the whole truth even about their own lives; they have disfigured the story that might have been so shapely. Facts are all that they can offer us, and facts are a very inferior form of fiction. Thus the desire grows upon us to have done with half-statements and approximations; to cease from searching out the minute shades of human character, to enjoy the greater abstractness, the purer truth of fiction. Thus we create the mood, intense and generalised, unaware of detail, but stressed by some regular, recurrent beat, whose natural expression is poetry; and that is the time to read poetry when we are almost able to write it.

Western wind, when wilt thou blow?
The small rain down can rain.
Christ, if my love were in my arms,
And I in my bed again!

The impact of poetry is so hard and direct that for the moment there is no other sensation except that of the poem itself. What profound depths we visit then—how sudden and complete is our immersion! There is nothing here to catch hold of; nothing to stay us in our flight. The illusion of fiction is gradual; its effects are prepared; but who when they read these four lines stops to ask who wrote them, or conjures up the thought of Donne's house or Sidney's secretary; or enmeshes them in the intricacy of the past and the succession of generations? The poet is always our contemporary. Our being for the moment is centred and constricted, as in any violent shock of personal emotion. Afterwards, it is true, the sensation begins to spread in wider rings through our minds; remoter senses are reached; these begin to sound and to comment and we are aware of echoes and reflections. The intensity of poetry covers an immense range of emotion. We have only to compare the force and directness of

> I shall fall like a tree, and find my grave,
> Only remembering that I grieve,

with the wavering modulation of

> Minutes are numbered by the fall of sands,
> As by an hour glass; the span of time
> Doth waste us to our graves, and we look on it;
> An age of pleasure, revelled out, comes home
> At last, and ends in sorrow; but the life,
> Weary of riot, numbers every sand,
> Wailing in sighs, until the last drop down,
> So to conclude calamity in rest,

or place the meditative calm of

> whether we be young or old,
> Our destiny, our being's heart and home,
> Is with infinitude, and only there;
> With hope it is, hope that can never die,
> Effort, and expectation, and desire,
> And something evermore about to be,

beside the complete and inexhaustible loveliness of

> The moving Moon went up the sky,
> And nowhere did abide:

Softly she was going up,
And a star or two beside—

or the splendid fantasy of

And the woodland haunter
Shall not cease to saunter
    When, far down some glade,
Of the great world's burning,
One soft flame upturning
Seems, to his discerning,
    Crocus in the shade,

to bethink us of the varied art of the poet; his
power to make us at once actors and spectators;
his power to run his hand into character as if it
were a glove, and be Falstaff or Lear; his power
to condense, to widen, to state, once and for ever.

"We have only to compare"—with those
words the cat is out of the bag, and the true com-
plexity of reading is admitted. The first process,
to receive impressions with the utmost understanding, is only half the process of reading; it
must be completed, if we are to get the whole

pleasure from a book, by another. We must pass judgment upon these multitudinous impressions; we must make of these fleeting shapes one that is hard and lasting. But not directly. Wait for the dust of reading to settle; for the conflict and the questioning to die down; walk, talk, pull the dead petals from a rose, or fall asleep. Then suddenly without our willing it, for it is thus that Nature undertakes these transitions, the book will return, but differently. It will float to the top of the mind as a whole. And the book as a whole is different from the book received currently in separate phrases. Details now fit themselves into their places. We see the shape from start to finish; it is a barn, a pig-sty, or a cathedral. Now then we can compare book with book as we compare building with building. But this act of comparison means that our attitude has changed; we are no longer the friends of the writer, but his judges; and just as we cannot be too sympathetic as friends, so as judges we cannot be too severe. Are they not criminals, books that have wasted our time and sympathy; are they not the most insidious enemies of society, corrupters, defilers, the writers of false books, faked books, books that fill the air with decay and disease? Let us then be severe in our judgments; let us compare each book with the greatest of its kind. There they hang in the mind the shapes of the books we have read solidified by the judgments we have passed on them—*Robinson Crusoe, Emma, The Return of the Native*. Compare the novels with these— even the latest and least of novels has a right to be judged with the best. And so with poetry—when the intoxication of rhythm has died down and the splendour of words has faded, a visionary shape will return to us and this must be compared with *Lear*, with *Phèdre*, with *The Prelude*; or if not with these, with whatever is the best or seems to us to be the best in its own kind. And we may be sure that the newness of new poetry and fiction is its most superficial quality and that we have only to alter slightly, not to recast, the standards by which we have judged the old.

It would be foolish, then, to pretend that the second part of reading, to judge, to compare, is as simple as the first—to open the mind wide to the fast flocking of innumerable impressions.

To continue reading without the book before you, to hold one shadow-shape against another, to have read widely enough and with enough understanding to make such comparisons alive and illuminating—that is difficult; it is still more difficult to press further and to say, "Not only is the book of this sort, but it is of this value; here it fails; here it succeeds; this is bad; that is good". To carry out this part of a reader's duty needs such imagination, insight, and learning that it is hard to conceive any one mind sufficiently endowed; impossible for the most self-confident to find more than the seeds of such powers in himself. Would it not be wiser, then, to remit this part of reading and to allow the critics, the gowned and furred authorities of the library, to decide the question of the book's absolute value for us? Yet how impossible! We may stress the value of sympathy; we may try to sink our own identity as we read. But we know that we cannot sympathise wholly or immerse ourselves wholly; there is always a demon in us who whispers, "I hate, I love", and we cannot silence him. Indeed, it is precisely because we hate and we love that our relation with the poets and novelists is so intimate that we find the presence of another person intolerable. And even if the results are abhorrent and our judgments are wrong, still our taste, the nerve of sensation that sends shocks through us, is our chief illuminant; we learn through feeling; we cannot suppress our own idiosyncrasy without impoverishing it. But as time goes on perhaps we can train our taste; perhaps we can make it submit to some control. When it has fed greedily and lavishly upon books of all sorts—poetry, fiction, history, biography—and has stopped reading and looked for long spaces upon the variety, the incongruity of the living world, we shall find that it is changing a little; it is not so greedy, it is more reflective. It will begin to bring us not merely judgments on particular books, but it will tell us that there is a quality common to certain books. Listen, it will say, what shall we call *this*? And it will read us perhaps *Lear* and then perhaps the *Agamemnon* in order to bring out that common quality. Thus, with our taste to guide us, we shall venture beyond the particular book in search of qualities that group books together; we shall give them names and thus frame a rule that brings order into our perceptions. We shall gain a further and a rarer pleasure from that discrimination. But as a rule only lives when it is perpetually broken by contact with the books themselves—nothing is easier and more stultifying than to make rules which exist out of touch with facts, in a vacuum—now at last, in order to steady ourselves in this difficult attempt, it may be well to turn to the very rare writers who are able to enlighten us upon literature as an art. Coleridge and Dryden and Johnson, in their considered criticism, the poets and novelists themselves in their unconsidered sayings, are often surprisingly relevant; they light up and solidify the vague ideas that have been tumbling in the misty depths of our minds. But they are only able to help us if we come to them laden with questions and suggestions won honestly in the course of our own reading. They can do nothing for us if we herd ourselves under their authority and lie down like sheep in the shade of a hedge. We can only understand their ruling when it comes in conflict with our own and vanquishes it.

If this is so, if to read a book as it should be read calls for the rarest qualities of imagination, insight, and judgment, you may perhaps conclude that literature is a very complex art and that it is unlikely that we shall be able, even after a life-time of reading, to make any valuable contribution to its criticism. We must remain readers; we shall not put on the further glory that belongs to those rare beings who are also critics. But still we have our responsibilities as readers and even our importance. The standards we raise and the judgments we pass steal into the air and become part of the atmosphere which writers breathe as they work. An influence is created which tells upon them even if it never finds its way into print. And that influence, if it were well instructed, vigorous and individual and sincere, might be of great value now when criticism is necessarily in abeyance; when books pass in review like the procession of animals in a shooting gallery, and the critic has only one second in which to load and aim and shoot and may well be pardoned if he mistakes rabbits for tigers, eagles for barn-door fowls, or misses altogether and wastes his shot upon some peaceful cow grazing in a further field. If behind the erratic gunfire of the press the author felt that there was another kind of criticism, the opinion of people reading for the love of reading, slowly and unprofessionally, and judging with great sympathy and yet with great severity, might this not improve the quality of his work? And if by our means books were to become stronger, richer, and more varied, that would be an end worth reaching.

Yet who reads to bring about an end, however desirable? Are there not some pursuits that we practise because they are good in themselves, and some pleasures that are final? And is not this among them? I have sometimes dreamt, at least, that when the Day of Judgment dawns and the great conquerors and lawyers and statesmen come to receive their rewards—their crowns, their laurels, their names carved indelibly upon imperishable marble—the Almighty will turn to Peter and will say, not without a certain envy when He sees us coming with our books under our arms, "Look, these need no reward. We have nothing to give them here. They have loved reading."

LETTER FROM CHARLES DICKENS TO WILKIE COLLINS, 1852

CHARLES DICKENS (1812–1870) was one of the founder members of The London Library. He wrote *A Tale of Two Cities* after Thomas Carlyle (the Library's founder) sent him a collection of the Library's books about the French Revolution.

WILKIE COLLINS (1824–1889) and Charles Dickens were firm friends, who first met in 1851 when the former acted in one of Dickens's amateur theatrical productions. It was Dickens who first serialised *The Woman in White*. Collins's novel *Basil: a Story of Modern Life* shocked the public with its themes of sexuality and madness.

MY DEAR COLLINS,

If I did not know that you are likely to have a forbearing remembrance of my occupation, I should be full of remorse for not having sooner thanked you for "Basil."

Not to play the sage or the critic (neither of which parts, I hope, is at all in my line), but to say what is the friendly truth, I may assure you that I have read the book with very great interest, and with a very thorough conviction that you have a call to this same art of fiction. I think the probabilities here and there require a little more respect than you are disposed to show them, and I have no doubt that the prefatory letter would have been better away, on the ground that a book (of all things) should speak for and explain itself. But the story contains admirable writing, and many clear evidences of a very delicate discrimination of character. It is delightful to find throughout that you have taken great pains with it besides, and have "gone at it" with a perfect knowledge of the jolter-headedness of the conceited idiots who suppose that volumes are to be tossed off like pancakes, and that any writing can be done without the utmost application, the greatest patience, and the steadiest energy of which the writer is capable.

For all these reasons I have made "Basil's" acquaintance with great gratification, and entertain a high respect for him. And I hope that I shall become intimate with many worthy descendants of his, who are yet in the limbo of creatures waiting to be born.

Always faithfully yours.

P.S.—I am open to any proposal to go anywhere any day or days this week. Fresh air and change in any amount I am ready for. If I could only find an idle man (this is a general observation), he would find the warmest recognition in this direction.

LETTER FROM CHARLES DICKENS TO GEORGE ELIOT, 1858

CHARLES DICKENS had the highest admiration for GEORGE ELIOT, who was still assumed to be a man when her 1858 book *Scenes of Clerical Life* was sent by her publishers to the leading authors of the day. She was deeply touched by Dickens's letter to her, and wrote to her publisher: "There can hardly be any climax of approbation for me after this; and I am so deeply moved by the finely-felt and finely-expressed sympathy of the letter."

MY DEAR SIR,—I have been so
strongly affected by the two first tales in the book
you have had the kindness to send me, through
Messrs Blackwood, that I hope you will excuse
my writing to you to express my admiration of
their extraordinary merit. The exquisite truth
and delicacy, both of the humour and the pathos
of these stories, I have never seen the like of; and
they have impressed me in a manner that I should
find it very difficult to describe to you, if I had
the impertinence to try.

In addressing these few words of thankful-
ness to the creator of the Sad Fortunes of the
Rev. Amos Barton, and the sad love-story of Mr
Gilfil, I am (I presume) bound to adopt the name
that it pleases that excellent writer to assume. I
can suggest no better one: but I should have been

strongly disposed, if I had been left to my own devices, to address the said writer as a woman. I have observed what seemed to me such womanly touches in those moving fictions, that the assurance on the title-page is insufficient to satisfy me even now. If they originated with no woman, I believe that no man ever before had the art of making himself mentally so like a woman since the world began.

You will not suppose that I have any vulgar wish to fathom your secret. I mention the point as one of great interest to me—not of mere curiosity. If it should ever suit your convenience and inclination to show me the face of the man, or woman, who has written so charmingly, it will be a very memorable occasion to me. If otherwise, I shall always hold that impalpable personage in loving attachment and respect, and shall yield myself up to all future utterances from the same source, with a perfect confidence in their making me wiser and better.—Your obliged and faithful servant and admirer,

CHARLES DICKENS.

AUTHORSHIP

Published in 1884

BY GEORGE ELIOT

GEORGE ELIOT (1819–1880) and George Henry Lewes, the man with whom she lived from 1854 until his death in 1878, were both devoted members of The London Library. (Lewes was also a member of the Committee from 1867–1878.) She was one of the greatest Victorian writers, whose novel *Middlemarch* was described by Virginia Woolf as "one of the few English novels written for grown-up people".

To lay down in the shape of practical moral rules courses of conduct only to be made real by the rarest states of motive and disposition, tends not to elevate but to degrade the general standard, by turning that rare attainment from an object of admiration into an impossible prescription, against which the average nature first rebels and then flings out ridicule. It is for art to present images of a lovelier order than the actual, gently winning the affections, and so determining the taste. But in any rational criticism of the time which is meant to guide a practical reform, it is idle to insist that action ought to be this or that, without considering how far the outward conditions of such change are present, even supposing the inward disposition towards it. Practically, we must be satisfied to aim at something short of perfection——and at something very much further off it in one case than in another. While the fundamental conceptions of morality seem as stationary through ages as the laws of life, so that a moral manual written eighteen centuries ago still admonishes us that we are low in our attainments, it is quite otherwise with the degree to which moral conceptions have penetrated the various forms of social activity, and made what may be called the special conscience of each calling, art, or industry. While on some points of social duty public opinion has reached a tolerably high standard, on others a public opinion is not yet born; and there are even some functions and practices with regard to which men far above the line in honourableness of nature feel hardly any scrupulosity, though their consequent behaviour is easily shown to be as injurious as bribery, or any other slowly poisonous procedure which degrades the social vitality.

Among those callings which have not yet acquired anything near a full-grown conscience in the public mind is Authorship. Yet the changes brought about by the spread of instruction and the consequent struggles of an uneasy ambition, are, or at least might well be, forcing on many minds the need of some regulating principle with regard to the publication of intellectual products, which would override the rule of the market: a principle, that is, which should be derived from a fixing of the author's vocation according to those characteristics in which it differs from the other bread-winning professions. Let this be done, if possible, without any cant, which would carry the subject into Utopia away from existing needs. The guidance wanted is a clear notion of what should justify men and women in assuming public authorship, and of the way in which they should be determined by what is usually called success. But the forms of authorship must be distinguished; journalism, for example, carrying a necessity for that continuous production which in other kinds of writing is precisely the evil to be fought against, and judicious careful compilation, which is a great public service, holding in its modest diligence a guarantee against those deductions of vanity and idleness which draw many a young gentleman into reviewing, instead of the sorting and copying which his small talents could not rise to with any vigour and completeness.

A manufacturer goes on producing calicoes as long and as fast as he can find a market for them; and in obeying this indication of demand he gives his factory its utmost usefulness to the world in general and to himself in particular. Another manufacturer buys a new invention of some light kind likely to attract the public fancy, is successful in finding a multitude who will give their testers for the transiently desirable commodity, and before the fashion is out, pockets a considerable sum: the commodity was coloured with a green which had arsenic in it that damaged the factory workers and the purchasers. What then? These, he contends (or does not know or care to contend), are superficial effects, which it is folly to dwell upon while we have epidemic diseases and bad government.

The first manufacturer we will suppose blameless. Is an author simply on a par with him, as to the rules of production?

The author's capital is his brain-power—power of invention, power of writing. The manufacturer's capital, in fortunate cases, is being continually reproduced and increased. Here is the first grand difference between the capital which is turned into calico and the brain capital which is turned into literature. The calico scarcely varies in appropriateness of quality, no consumer is in danger of getting too much of it, and neglecting his boots, hats, and flannel-shirts in consequence. That there should be large quantities of the same sort in the calico manufacture is an advantage: the sameness is desirable, and nobody is likely to roll his person in so many folds of calico as to become a mere bale of cotton goods, and nullify his senses of hearing and touch, while his morbid passion for Manchester shirtings makes him still cry "More!" The wise manufacturer gets richer and richer, and the consumers he supplies have their real wants satisfied and no more.

Let it be taken as admitted that all legitimate social activity must be beneficial to others besides the agent. To write prose or verse as a private exercise and satisfaction is not social activity; nobody is culpable for this any more than for learning other people's verse by heart if he does not neglect his proper business in consequence. If the exercise made him sillier or secretly more self-satisfied, that, to be sure, would be a round-about way of injuring society; for though a certain mixture of silliness may lighten existence, we have at present more than enough.

But man or woman who publishes writings inevitably assumes the office of teacher or influencer of the public mind. Let him protest as he will that he only seeks to amuse, and has no pretension to do more than while away an hour of leisure or weariness—"the idle singer of an empty day"—he can no more escape influencing the moral taste, and with it the action of the intelligence, than a setter of fashions in furniture and dress can fill the shops with his designs and leave the garniture of persons and houses unaffected by his industry.

For a man who has a certain gift of writing to say, "I will make the most of it while the public likes my wares—as long as the market is open and I am able to supply it at a money profit—such profit being the sign of liking"—he should have a belief that his wares have nothing akin to the arsenic green in them, and also that his continuous supply is secure from a degradation in quality which the habit of consumption encouraged in the buyers may hinder them from marking their sense of by rejection; so that they complain, but pay, and read while they complain. Unless he has that belief, he is on a level with the manufacturer who gets rich by fancy-wares coloured with arsenic green. He really cares for nothing but his income. He carries on authorship on the principle of the gin-palace.

And bad literature of the sort called amusing is spiritual gin.

A writer capable of being popular can only escape this social culpability by first of all getting a profound sense that literature is good-for-nothing, if it is not admirably good: he must detest bad literature too heartily to be indifferent about producing it if only other people don't detest it. And if he has this sign of the divine afflatus within him, he must make up his mind that he must not pursue authorship as a vocation with a trading determination to get rich by it. It is in the highest sense lawful for him to get as good a price as he honourably can for the best work he is capable of; but not for him to force or hurry his production, or even do over again what has already been done, either by himself or others, so as to render his work no real contribution, for the sake of bringing up his income to the fancy pitch. An author who would keep a pure and noble conscience, and with that a developing instead of degenerating intellect and taste, must cast out of his aims the aim to be rich. And therefore he must keep his expenditure low—he must make for himself no dire necessity to earn sums in order to pay bills.

In opposition to this, it is common to cite Walter Scott's case, and cry, "Would the world have got as much innocent (and therefore salutary) pleasure out of Scott, if he had not brought himself under the pressure of money-need?" I think it would—and more; but since it is impossible to prove what would have been, I confine myself to replying that Scott was not justified in bringing himself into a position where severe consequences to others depended on his retaining or not retaining his mental competence. Still less is Scott to be taken as an example to be followed in this matter, even if it were admitted that money-need served to press at once the best and the most work out of him; any more than a great navigator who has brought his ship to port in spite of having taken a wrong and perilous route, is to be followed as to his route by navigators who are not yet ascertained to be great.

But after the restraints and rules which must guide the acknowledged author, whose power of making a real contribution is ascertained, comes the consideration, how or on what principle are we to find a check for that troublesome disposition to authorship arising from the spread of what is called Education, which turns a growing rush of vanity and ambition into this current? The well-taught, an increasing number, are almost all able to write essays on given themes, which demand new periodicals to save them from lying in cold obstruction. The ill-taught—also an increasing number—read many books, seem to themselves able to write others surprisingly like what they read, and probably superior, since the variations are such as please their own fancy, and such as they would have recommended to their favourite authors: these ill-taught persons are perhaps idle and want to give themselves "an object"; or they are short of money, and feel disinclined to get it by a commoner kind of work; or they find a facility in putting sentences together which gives them more than a suspicion that they have genius, which, if not very cordially believed in by private confidants, will be recognised by an impartial public; or finally, they observe that writing is sometimes well paid, and sometimes a ground of fame or distinction, and without any use of punctilious logic, they conclude to become writers themselves.

As to these ill-taught persons, whatever medicines of a spiritual sort can be found good against mental emptiness and inflation—such medicines are needful for *them*. The contempt of the world for their productions only comes after their disease has wrought its worst effects. But what is to be said to the well-taught, who have such an alarming equality in their power of writing "like a scholar and a gentleman"? Perhaps they, too, can only be cured by the medicine of higher ideals in social duty, and by a fuller representation to themselves of the processes by which the general culture is furthered or impeded.

MY BOOKS

Published in 1899

BY LEIGH HUNT

James Henry Leigh Hunt (1784–1859) was the 877th person to join The London Library. He was a poet, critic and journalist, who founded the radical weekly *The Examiner*. In 1813, he was sent to Horsemonger Lane gaol for two years for writing an article condemning the Prince Regent. Despite being a household name in his day, and remembered as one of the great reformers, his poetry has not been widely read.

Sitting, last winter, among my books, and walled round with all the comfort and protection which they and my fireside could afford me; to wit, a table of high-piled books at my back, my writing-desk on one side of me, some shelves on the other, and the feeling of the warm fire at my feet; I began to consider how I loved the authors of those books,—how I loved them, too, not only for the imaginative pleasures they afforded me, but for their making me love the very books themselves, and delight to be in contact with them. I looked sideways at my *Spenser*, my *Theocritus*, and my *Arabian Nights*; then above them at my Italian poets; then behind me at my *Dryden* and *Pope*, my romances, and my *Boccaccio*; then on my left side at my *Chaucer*, who lay on a writing-desk; and thought how natural it was in C.L. to give a kiss to an old folio, as I once saw him do to Chapman's *Homer*. At the same time I wondered how he could sit in that front room of his with nothing but a few unfeeling tables and chairs, or at best a few engravings in trim frames, instead of putting a couple of arm-chairs into the back-room with the books in it, where there is but one window. Would I were there, with both the chairs properly filled, and one or two more besides! "We had talk, sir"——the only talk capable of making one forget the books.

I entrench myself in my books equally against sorrow and the weather. If the wind comes through a passage, I look about to see how I can fence it off by a better disposition of my movables; if a melancholy thought is importunate, I give another glance at my *Spenser*. When I speak of being in contact with my books, I mean it literally. I like to lean my head against them. Living in a southern climate, though in a part sufficiently northern to feel the winter, I was obliged, during that season, to take some of the books out of the study, and hang them up near the fireplace in the sitting-room, which is the only room that has such a convenience. I therefore walled myself in, as well as I could, in the manner above mentioned. I took a walk every day, to the astonishment of the Genoese, who used to huddle against a piece of sunny wall, like flies on a chimney-piece; but I did this only that I might so much the more enjoy my *English* evening. The fire was a wood fire instead of a coal; but I imagined myself in the country. I remember at the very worst that one end of my native land was not nearer the other than England is to Italy.

While writing this article I am in my study again. Like the rooms in all houses in this country which are not hovels, it is handsome and orna-mented. On one side it looks towards a garden and the mountains; on another to the mountains and the sea. What signifies all this? I turn my back upon the sea; I shut up even one of the side win-dows looking upon the mountains, and retain no prospect but that of the trees. On the right and left of me are book-shelves; a bookcase is affec-tionately open in front of me; and thus kindly enclosed with my books and the green leaves, I write. If all this is too luxurious and effeminate, of all luxuries it is the one that leaves you the most strength. And this is to be said for scholarship in general. It unfits a man for activity, for his bodily part in the world; but it often doubles both the power and the sense of his mental duties; and with much indignation against his body, and more against those who tyrannise over the intellectual claims of mankind, the man of letters, like the magician of old, is prepared "to play the devil" with the great men of this world, in a style that astonishes both the sword and the toga.

I do not like this fine large study. I like elegance. I like room to breathe in, and even walk about, when I want to breathe and walk about. I like a great library next my study; but for the study itself, give me a small snug place, almost entirely walled with books. There should be only one window in it, looking upon trees. Some prefer a place with few or no books at all—nothing but a chair or a table, like Epictetus; but I should say that these were philosophers, not lovers of books, if I did not recollect that Montaigne was both. He had a study in a round tower, walled as aforesaid. It is true, one forgets one's books while writing— at least they say so. For my part, I think none— like a waterfall or a whispering wind.

I dislike a grand library to study in. I mean an immense apartment, with books all in Museum order, especially wire-safed. I say nothing against the Museum itself, or public libraries. They are capital places to go to, but not to sit in; and talking of this, I hate to read in public, and in strange company. The jealous silence; the dissatisfied looks of the messengers; the inability to help yourself; the not knowing whether you really ought to trouble the messengers, much less the *gentleman* in black, or brown, who is, perhaps, half a trustee; with a variety of other jarrings between privacy and publicity, prevent one's settling heartily to work. They say "they manage these things better in France"; and I dare say they do; but I think I should feel still more *distrait* in France, in spite of the benevolence of the servitors, and the generous profusion of pen, ink, and paper. I should feel as if I were doing nothing but interchanging amenities with polite writers.

A grand private library, which the master of the house also makes his study, never looks to me like a real place of books, much less of authorship. I cannot take kindly to it. It is certainly not out of envy; for three parts of the books are generally trash, and I can seldom think of the rest and the proprietor together. It reminds me of a fine gentleman, of a collector, of a patron, of Gil Blas and the Marquis of Marialva; of anything but genius and comfort. I have a particular hatred of a round table (not *the* Round Table, for that was a dining one) covered and irradiated with books, and never met with one in the house of a clever man but once. It is the reverse of Montaigne's Round Tower. Instead of bringing the books around you, they all seem turning another way, and eluding your hands.

Conscious of my propriety and comfort in these matters, I take an interest in the bookcases as well as the books of my friends. I long to meddle and dispose them after my own notions. When they see this confession, they will acknowledge the virtue I have practised. I believe I did mention his book-room to C.L., and I think he told me that he often sat there when alone. It would be hard not to believe him. His library, though not abounding in Greek or Latin (which are the only things to help some persons to an idea of literature), is anything but superficial. The depth of philosophy and poetry are there, the innermost passages of

the human heart. It has some Latin too. It has
also a handsome contempt for appearance. It
looks like what it is, a selection made at precious
intervals from the bookstalls; now a Chaucer at
nine and twopence; now a Montaigne or a Sir
Thomas Browne at two shillings; now a Jeremy
Taylor; a Spinoza; an old English Dramatist,
Prior, and Sir Philip Sidney; and the books are
"neat as imported." The very perusal of the backs
is a "discipline of humanity." There Mr. Southey
takes his place again with an old Radical friend:
there Jeremy Collier is at peace with Dryden:
there the lion, Martin Luther, lies down with
the Quaker lamb, Sewell: there Guzman d'Al-
farache thinks himself fit company for Sir Charles
Grandison, and has his claims admitted. Even the
"high fantastical" Duchess of Newcastle, with
her laurel on her head, is received with grave
honours, and not the less for declining to trouble herself with the constitutions of her maids.
There is an approach to this in the library of W.C.
who also includes Italian among his humanities.
W.H., I believe, has no books, except mine; but
he has Shakespeare and Rousseau by heart. N.,

who, though not a bookman by profession, is fond of those who are, and who loves his volume enough to read it across the fields, has his library in the common sitting-room, which is hospitable. H.R.'s books are all too modern and finely bound, which, however, is not his fault, for they were left him by will—not the most kindly act of the testator. Suppose a man were to bequeath us a great japan chest three feet by four, with an injunction that it was always to stand on the tea-table. I remember borrowing a book of H.R., which, having lost, I replaced with a copy equally well bound. I am not sure I should have been in such haste, even to return the book, had it been a common-looking volume; but the splendour of the loss dazzled me into this ostentatious piece of propriety. I set about restoring it as if I had diminished his fortunes, and waived the privilege a friend has to use a man's things as his own. I may venture upon this ultra-liberal theory, not only because candour compels me to say that I hold it to a greater extent, with Montaigne, but because I have been a meek son in the family of book-losers. I may affirm, upon a moderate calculation, that I have lent and lost in my time (and I am eight-and-thirty), half a dozen decent-sized libraries—I mean books enough to fill so many ordinary bookcases. I have never complained; and self-love, as well as gratitude, makes me love those who do not complain of me.

I own I borrow books with as much facility as I lend. I cannot see a work that interests me on another person's shelf, without a wish to carry it off; but, I repeat, that I have been much more sinned against than sinning in the article of non-return; and am scrupulous in the article of intention. I never had a felonious intent upon a book but once; and then I shall only say, it was under circumstances so peculiar, that I cannot but look upon the conscience that induced me to restore it, as having sacrificed the spirit of its very self to the letter; and I have a grudge against it accordingly. Some people are unwilling to lend their books. I have a special grudge against them, particularly those who accompany their unwillingness with uneasy professions to the contrary, and smiles like Sir Fretful Plagiary. The friend who helped to spoil my notions of property, or rather to make them too good for the world "as it goes," taught me also to undervalue my squeamishness in refusing to avail myself of the books of these gentlemen. He showed me how it was doing good to all parties to put an ordinary face on the matter; though I know his own blushed not a little sometimes in doing it, even when the good to be done was for another. I feel, in truth, that even when anger inclines me to exercise this privilege of philosophy, it is more out of revenge than contempt. I fear that in allowing myself to borrow books, I sometimes make extremes meet in a very sinful manner, and do it out of a refined revenge. It is like eating a miser's beef at him.

I yield to none in my love of bookstall urbanity. I have spent as happy moments over the stalls as any literary apprentice boy who ought to be moving onwards. But I confess my weakness in liking to see some of my favourite purchases neatly bound. The books I like to have about me most are——Spenser, Chaucer, the minor poems of Milton, the *Arabian Nights*, Theocritus, Ariosto, and such old good-natured speculations as Plutarch's *Morals*. For most of these I like a plain, good, old binding, never mind how old, provided it wears well; but my *Arabian Nights* may be bound in as fine and flowery a style as possible, and I should love an engraving to every dozen pages. Bookprints of all sorts, bad and good, take with me as much as when I was a child; and I think some books, such as Prior's *Poems*, ought always to have portraits of the authors. Prior's airy face with his cap on is like having his company. From early association, no edition of Milton pleases me so much as that in which there are pictures of the Devil with brute ears, dressed like a Roman General: nor of Bunyan, as the one containing the print of the Valley of the Shadow of Death, with the Devil whispering in Christian's ear, or old Pope by the wayside, and

Vanity Fair,
With the Pilgrims suffering there.

I delight in the recollection of the puzzle I used to have with the frontispiece of the *Tale of a Tub*, of my real horror at the sight of that crawling old man, representing Avarice, at the beginning of *Enfield's Speaker*, the *Looking-Glass*, or some such book; and even of the careless school-boy hats, and the prim stomachers and cottage bonnets, of such golden-age antiquities as the *Village School*. The oldest and most worn-out woodcut, representing King Pippin, Goody Two Shoes, or the grim Soldan, sitting with three staring blots for his eyes and mouth, his sceptre in one hand, and his other five fingers raised and spread in admiration at the feats of the Gallant London 'Prentice, cannot excite in me a feeling of ingratitude. Cooke's edition of the *British Poets and Novelists* came out when I was at school: for which reason I never could put up with Suttaby's or Walker's publications, except in the case of such works as the *Fairy Tales*: which Mr. Cooke did not publish. Besides, they are too cramped, thick, and mercenary; and the pictures are all frontispieces. They do not come in at the proper places. Cooke realised the old woman's *beau ideal* of a prayer-book—"A little book, with a great deal of matter, and a large type":—for the type was really large for so small a volume. Shall I ever forget his Collins and his

Gray, books at once so "superbly ornamented"
and so inconceivably cheap? Sixpence could procure much before; but never could it procure so
much as then, or was at once so much respected,
and so little cared for. His artist Kirk was the
best artist, except Stothard, that ever designed
for periodical works; and I will venture to add
(if his name rightly announces his country) the
best artist Scotland ever produced, except Wilkie,
but he unfortunately had not enough of his country in him to keep him from dying young. His
designs for Milton and the *Arabian Nights*, his
female extricated from the water in the *Tales of
the Genii*, and his old hag issuing out of the chest
of the Merchant Abadah in the same book, are
before me now, as vividly as they were then. He
possessed elegance and the sense of beauty in no
ordinary degree; though they sometimes played
a trick or so of foppery. I shall never forget the
gratitude with which I received an odd number
of Akenside, value sixpence, one of the set of that
poet, which a boarder distributed among three
or four of us, "with his mother's compliments."
The present might have been more lavish, but I

hardly thought of that. I remember my number. It was the one in which there was a picture of the poet on a sofa, with Cupid coming to him, and the words underneath, "Tempt me no more, insidious love!" The picture and the number appeared to me equally divine. I cannot help thinking to this day, that it is right and natural in a gentleman to sit in a stage dress, on that particular kind of sofa, though on no other, with that exclusive hat and feathers on his head, telling Cupid to be gone, with a tragic air.

I love an author the more for having been himself a lover of books. The idea of an ancient library perplexes our sympathy by its map-like volumes, rolled upon cylinders. Our imagination cannot take kindly to a yard of wit, or to thirty inches of moral observation, rolled out like linen in a draper's shop. But we conceive of Plato as of a lover of books; of Aristotle certainly; of Plutarch, Pliny, Horace, Julian, and Marcus Aurelius. Virgil, too, must have been one; and, after a fashion, Martial. May I confess, that the passage which I recollect with the greatest pleasure in Cicero is where he says that books delight us at home, *and are no impediment abroad*; travel with us, ruralise with us. His period is rounded off to some purpose: "*Delectant domi, non impediunt foris; peregrinantur, rusticantur.*" I am so much of this opinion that I do not care to be anywhere without having a book or books at hand, and, like Dr. Orkborne, in the novel of *Camilla*, stuff the coach or post-chaise with them whenever I travel. As books, however, become ancient, the love of them becomes more unequivocal and con-spicuous. The ancients had little of what we call learning. They made it. They were also no very eminent buyers of books—they made books for posterity. It is true, that it is not at all necessary to love many books, in order to love them much. The scholar, in Chaucer, who would rather have

> At his beddes head
> A twenty bokes, clothed in black and red,
> Of Aristotle and his philosophy,
> Than robès rich, or fiddle, or psaltrie,

doubtless beat all our modern collectors in his pas-sion for reading; but books must at least exist, and have acquired an eminence, before their lovers can make themselves known. There must be a possession, also, to perfect the communion; and the mere contact is much, even when our mistress speaks an unknown language. Dante puts Homer, the great ancient, in his *Elysium* upon trust; but a few years afterwards, *Homer*, the book, made its appearance in Italy, and Petrarch, in a transport, put it upon his book-shelves, where he adored it, like "the unknown God." Petrarch ought to be the god of the bibliomaniacs, for he was a collector and a man of genius, which is a union that does not often happen. He copied out, with his own precious hand, the manuscripts he rescued from time, and then produced others for time to reverence. With his head upon a book he died. Boccaccio, his friend, was another; nor can one look upon the longest and most tiresome works he wrote (for he did write some tiresome ones, in spite of the gaiety of his *Decameron*), without thinking, that in that resuscitation of the world of letters it must have been natural to a man of genius to add to the existing stock of volumes, at whatsoever price. I always pitch my completest idea of a lover of books, either in those dark ages, as they are called—

(Cui cieco a torto il cieco volgo appella)—

or in the gay town days of Charles II., or a little afterwards. In both times the portrait comes out by the force of contrast. In the first, I imagine an age of iron warfare and energy, with solitary retreats, in which the monk or the hooded scholar walks forth to meditate, his precious volume under his arm. In the other, I have a triumphant example of the power of books and wit to contest the victory with sensual pleasure:— Rochester, staggering home to pen a satire in the style of Monsieur Boileau; Butler, cramming his jolly duodecimo with all the learning that he laughed at; and a new race of book poets come up, who, in spite of their periwigs and *petits-maîtres*, talk as romantically of "the bays" as if they were priests of Delphos. It was a victorious thing in books to beguile even the old French of their egotism, or at least to share it with them. Nature never pretended to do as much. And here is the difference between the two ages, or between any two ages in which genius and art predominate. In the one, books are loved because they are the records of Nature and her energies; in the other, because they are the records of those records, or evidences of the importance of the individuals, and proofs of our descent in the new imperishable aristocracy. This is the reason why rank (with few exceptions) is so jealous of literature, and loves to appropriate or withhold the honours of it, as if they were so many toys and ribbons, like its own. It has an instinct that the two pretensions are incompatible. When Montaigne (a real lover of books) affected the order of St. Michael, and pleased himself with possessing that fugitive little piece of importance, he did it because he would pretend to be above nothing that he really felt, or that was felt by men in general; but at the same time he vindicated his natural superiority over this weakness by praising and loving all higher and lasting things, and by placing his best glory in doing homage to the geniuses that had gone before him. He did not endeavour to think that an immortal renown was a fashion, like that of the cut of his scarf; or that by undervaluing the one, he should go shining down to posterity in the other, perpetual lord of Montaigne and of the ascendant.

There is a period of modern times, at which the love of books appears to have been of a more decided nature than at either of these—I mean the age just before and after the Reformation, or rather all that period when book-writing was confined to the learned languages. Erasmus is the god of it. Bacon, a mighty bookman, saw, among his other sights, the great advantage of loosening the vernacular tongue, and wrote both Latin and English. I allow this is the greatest closeted age of books; of old scholars sitting in dusty studies; of heaps of "illustrious obscure," rendering themselves more illustrious and more obscure by retreating from the "thorny queaches" of Dutch and German names into the "vacant interlunar caves" of appellations latinised or translated. I think I see all their volumes now, filling the shelves of a dozen German convents. The authors are bearded men, sitting in old woodcuts, in caps and gowns, and their books are dedicated to princes and statesmen, as illustrious as themselves. My old friend Wierus, who wrote a thick book, *De Praestigiis Daemonum*, was one of them, and had a fancy worthy of his sedentary stomach. I will confess, once for all, that I have a liking for them all. It is my link with the bibliomaniacs, whom I admit into our relationship, because my love is large, and my family pride nothing. But still I take my idea of books read with a gusto, of companions for bed and board, from the two ages before mentioned. The other is of too bookworm a description. There must be both a judgment and a fervour; a discrimination and a boyish eagerness; and (with all due humility) something of a point of contact between authors worth reading and the reader. How can I take Juvenal into the fields, or Valcarenghius *De Aortae Aneurismate* to bed with me? How could I expect to walk before the face of nature with the one; to tire my elbow properly with the other, before I put out my candle, and turn round deliciously on the right side? Or how could I stick up Coke upon

Littleton against something on the dinner-table, and be divided between a fresh paragraph and a mouthful of salad?

I take our four great English poets to have all been fond of reading. Milton and Chaucer proclaim themselves for hard sitters at books. Spenser's reading is evident by his learning; and if there were nothing else to show for it in Shakespeare, his retiring to his native town, long before old age, would be a proof of it. It is impossible for a man to live in solitude without such assistance, unless he is a metaphysician or mathematician, or the dullest of mankind; and any country town would be solitude to Shakespeare, after the bustle of a metropolis and a theatre. Doubtless he divided his time between his books, and his bowling-green, and his daughter Susanna. It is pretty certain, also, that he planted, and rode on horseback; and there is evidence of all sorts to make it clear, that he must have occasionally joked with the blacksmith, and stood godfather for his neighbours' children. Chaucer's account of himself must be quoted, for the delight and sympathy of all true readers:—

And as for me, though that I can but lite,
On bookès for to rede I me delite,
And to hem yeve I faith and full credènce,
And in mine herte have hem in reverence
So hertèly, that there is gamè none,
That fro my bookès maketh me to gone,
But it is seldome on the holy daie;
Save certainly whan that the month of May
Is comen, and that I hear the foulès sing,
And that the flourès ginnen for to spring.
Farewell my booke and my devociön.

                    The Legend of Good Women.

And again, in the second book of his *House of Fame*, where the *eagle* addresses him:—

                    Thou wilt make
At night full oft thine head to ake,
And in thy study as thou writest,
And evermore of Love enditest.
In honour of him and his praisings,
And in his folkès furtherings,
And in his matter all devisest,
And not him ne his folke despisest,

Although thou mayst go in the daunse
Of hem, that him list not advance;
Therefore as I said, ywis,
Jupiter considreth well this.
And also, beausire, of other things;
That is, thou hast no tidings
Of Lovès folke, if they be glade,
Ne of nothing else that God made,
And not only fro ferre countree,
But no tidings commen to thee,
Not of thy very neighbouris,
That dwellen almost at thy dores;
Thou hearest neither that ne this,
For whan thy labour all done is,
And hast made all thy rekenings,
Instead of rest and of new things,
Thou goest home to thine house anone,
And all so dombe as anie stone,
Thou sittest at another booke,
Till fully dazed is thy looke.

After I think of the bookishness of Chaucer and
Milton, I always make a great leap to Prior and
Fenton. Prior was first noticed, when a boy, by

Lord Dorset, sitting in his uncle's tavern, and reading Horace. He describes himself, years after, when Secretary of Embassy at the Hague, as taking the same author with him in the Saturday's chaise, in which he and his mistress used to escape from town cares into the country, to the admiration of Dutch beholders. Fenton was a martyr to contented scholarship (including a sirloin and a bottle of wine), and died among his books, of inactivity. "He rose late," says Johnson, "and when he had risen, sat down to his books and papers." A woman that once waited on him in a lodging, told him, as she said, that he would "lie a-bed and be fed with a spoon." He must have had an enviable liver, if he was happy. I must own (if my conscience would let me), that I should like to lead, half the year, just such a life (woman included, though not that woman), the other half being passed in the fields and woods, with a cottage just big enough to hold us. Dacier and his wife had a pleasant time of it; both fond of books, both scholars, both amiable, both wrapt up in the ancient world, and helping one another at their tasks. If they were not happy, matrimony would be a rule even without an exception. Pope does not strike me as being a bookman; he was curious rather than enthusiastic; more nice than wise; he dabbled in modern Latin poetry, which is a bad symptom. Swift was decidedly a reader; the *Tale of a Tub*, in its fashion as well as substance, is the work of a scholarly wit; the *Battle of the Books* is the fancy of a lover of libraries. Addison and Steele were too much given up to Button's and the town. Periodical writing, though its demands seem otherwise, is not favourable to reading; it becomes too much a matter of business, and will either be attended to at the expense of the writer's books, or books, the very admonishers of his industry, will make him idle. Besides, a periodical work, to be suitable to its character, and warrant its regular recurrence, must involve something of a gossiping nature, and proceed upon experiences familiar to the existing community, or at least likely to be received by them in consequence of some previous tinge of inclination. You do not pay weekly visits to your friends to lecture them, whatever good you may do their minds. There will be something compulsory in reading the *Ramblers*, as there is in going to church. Addison and Steele undertook to regulate the minor morals of society, and effected a world of good, with which scholarship had little to do. Gray was a bookman; he wished to be always lying on sofas, reading "eternal new novels of Crebillon and Marivaux." This is a true hand. The elaborate and scientific look of the rest of his reading was owing to the necessity of employing himself: he had not health and spirits for the literary voluptuousness he desired. Collins, for the same reason, could not employ himself; he was obliged to dream over Arabian tales, to let the light of the supernatural world half in upon his eyes. "He loved," as Johnson says (in that strain of music, inspired by tenderness), "fairies, genii, giants, and monsters; he delighted to rove through the meanders of enchantment, to gaze on the magnificence of golden palaces, to repose by the waterfalls of Elysian gardens." If Collins had had a better constitution, I do not believe that he would have written his projected work upon the *Restoration of Literature*, fit as he was by scholarship for the task, but he would have been

the greatest poet since the days of Milton. If his
friend Thomas Warton had had a little more of his
delicacy of organisation, the love of books would
almost have made him a poet. His edition of the
minor poems of Milton is a wilderness of sweets. It
is the only one in which a true lover of the original
can pardon an exuberance of annotation; though I
confess I am inclined enough to pardon any notes
that resemble it, however numerous. The "builded
rhyme" stands at the top of the page, like a fair
edifice, with all sorts of flowers and fresh waters
at its foot. The young poet lives there, served by the
nymphs and fauns.

Hinc atque hinc glomerantur Oreades.
Huc ades, o formose puer; tibi lilia plenis
Ecce ferunt nymphae calathis: tibi candida Nais
Pallentes violas et summa papavera carpens,
Narcissum et florem jungit bene olentis anethi.

Among the old writers I must not forget Ben Jonson
and Donne. Cowley has been already mentioned.
His boyish love of books, like all the other incli-
nations of his early life, stuck to him to the last,

which is the greatest reward of virtue. I would mention Izaak Walton, if I had not a grudge against him. His brother fishermen, the divines, were also great fishers of books. I have a grudge against them and their divinity. They talked much of the devil and divine right, and yet forgot what Shakespeare says of the devil's friend Nero, that he is "an angler in the lake of darkness." Selden was called "the walking library of our nation." It is not the pleasantest idea of him; but the library included poetry, and wit, as well as heraldry and the Jewish doctors. His *Table Talk* is equally pithy and pleasant, and truly worthy of the name, for it implies other speakers. Indeed, it was actually what it is called, and treasured up by his friends. Selden wrote complimentary verses to his friends the poets, and a commentary on Drayton's *Polyolbion*. Drayton was himself a reader, addicted to all the luxuries of scholarship. Chapman sat among his books, like an astrologer among his spheres and altitudes.

How pleasant it is to reflect, that all those lovers of books have themselves become books! What better metamorphosis could Pythagoras have desired? How Ovid and Horace exulted in anticipating theirs! And how the world have justi-fied their exultation! They had a right to triumph over brass and marble. It is the only visible change which changes no farther; which generates and yet is not destroyed. Consider: mines themselves are exhausted; cities perish; kingdoms are swept away, and man weeps with indignation to think that his own body is not immortal.

> Muoiono le città, muoiono i regni,
> E l'uom d'esser mortal par che si sdegni.

Yet this little body of thought, that lies before me in the shape of a book, has existed thousands of years, nor since the invention of the press can any-thing short of an universal convulsion of nature abolish it. To a shape like this, so small yet so comprehensive, so slight yet so lasting, so insignif-icant yet so venerable, turns the mighty activity of Homer, and so turning, is enabled to live and warm us for ever. To a shape like this turns the placid sage of Academus: to a shape like this the grandeur of Milton, the exuberance of Spenser, the pungent elegance of Pope, and the volatility of Prior. In one small room, like the compressed spirits of Milton, can be gathered together

The assembled souls of all that men held wise.

May I hope to become the meanest of these existences? This is a question which every author who is a lover of books asks himself some time in his life; and which must be pardoned, because it cannot be helped. I know not. I cannot exclaim with the poet,

Oh that my name were number'd among theirs,
Then gladly would I end my mortal days.

For my mortal days, few and feeble as the rest of them may be, are of consequence to others. But I should like to remain visible in this shape. The little of myself that pleases myself, I could wish to be accounted worth pleasing others. I should like to survive so, were it only for the sake of those who love me in private, knowing as I do what a treasure is the possession of a friend's mind when he is no more. At all events, nothing while I live and think can deprive me of my value for such treasures. I can help the appreciation of them while I last, and love them till I die; and perhaps, if fortune turns her face once more in kindness upon me before I go, I may chance, some quiet day, to lay my overheating temples on a book, and so have the death I most envy.

[This paper was written during Hunt's residence in Italy. The initials 'C.L.,' 'W.H.,' 'H.R.,' and 'N.' are those of Charles Lamb, William Hazlitt, Henry Robinson, and Vincent Novello.]

THE LONDON LIBRARY

First published in 1941

BY E.M. FORSTER

EDWARD MORGAN FORSTER (1879–1970) joined
The London Library in 1904 as a life member. He was
Vice-President from 1961 until his death. In 1960,
he donated his draft material and manuscript of *A
Passage to India* to the Library for its fund-raising
auction at Christie's, where it made £6,500—then a
record price for a manuscript by a living writer.

In May 1841 the London Library was launched on the swelling tides of Victorian prosperity. It celebrates its centenary among the rocks. It is unharmed at the moment of writing—not a volume out of action—but the area in which it stands is cloven by the impacts of the imbecile storm. All around it are the signs of the progress of science and the retrogression of man. Buildings are in heaps, the earth is in holes. Safe still among the reefs of rubbish, it seems to be something more than a collection of books. It is a symbol of civilisation. It is a reminder of sanity and a promise of sanity to come. Perhaps the Nazis will hit it, and it is an obvious target, for it represents the tolerance and the disinterested erudition which they so detest. But they have missed it so far.*

Why should a private subscription library, which appeals to only a small section of the

---

* They hit it in 1944.

community, arouse exalted thoughts? The answer to this question is to be found in the Library's history, and in its present policy. Speakers at its annual meetings are fond of saying that it is unique, which is more or less true, and that it is typically English, which greatly understates its claims. It is not typically English. It is typically civilised. It pays a homage to seriousness and to good sense which is rare in these islands and anywhere. It has cherished the things of the mind, it has insisted on including all points of view, and yet it has been selective. Ephemeral books, popular successes, most novels, many travelogues and biographies have been excluded from its shelves. And technical treatises, such as have helped to make the mess outside, have not been encouraged either. Of course it has had its lapses; one can find trash in it, and specialisation-lumber also. But its policy has always been to send those who want trash to the chain-libraries, and those who want lumber to their appropriate lumber-room. It caters neither for the goose nor for the rat, but for creatures who are trying to be human. The desire to know more, the desire to feel more, and, accompanying these but not strangling them, the desire to help others: here, briefly, is the human aim, and the Library exists to further it.

So much for its seriousness. Its good sense is equally remarkable. For it would be possible to have these admirable ideals, but to render them unacceptable through red-tape. That is the great snag in institutionalism. There may be fine intention and noble provision, but they often get spoiled by the belief that the public cannot be trusted, that it is careless, dishonest, grubby, clumsy, that it must on no account be "allowed access" to the shelves, and is best served from behind a wire netting. The London Library, though an institution, will have nothing to do with this fallacy. It takes the risks. Its members can go all over its book-stores. There is a price to be paid; books do get stolen, or taken out without being entered or taken out in unauthorised quantities, or kept out too long, or dogs-eared, or annotated in the margin by cultivated scribes who should know better; but it is worth it, it is worth treating the creatures as if they were grown up, the gain to the humanities outweighs the financial loss. Moreover, it is the tradition of the library to help the student rather than to snub, and this promotes a decent reaction at once. And "help" is indeed too feeble a word; the officials there possess not only good-will, but wide and accurate knowledge, which is instantly placed at the enquirer's disposal.

The library owes its origin to the spleen and to the nobility of Thomas Carlyle. The spleen came first; Carlyle needed books of reference while he was writing his *Cromwell*, he could not afford to buy them all, and the journey from Chelsea to the British Museum Library was a vexatious one. Besides, when he got to the British Museum he found other people reading there too, which gave him the feeling of a crowd, and it is impossible to work in a crowd: "add discomfort, perturbation, headache, waste of health." Grumbling and growling at his miserable fate, he betook himself to the drawing-room of Lady Stanley of Alderley in Dover Street, and burst forth there; even in Iceland, he said, the peasants could borrow books, and take them away to read in their huts during the Arctic night; only

in London was there this "shameful anomaly."
The company tried to soothe him or to change the
subject, but his growls continued; books, books,
one ought to be able to borrow books. And before
long, he effected one of his junctions between
private peevishness and public welfare, and per-
suaded other men of distinction to combine with
him in launching a library. Gladstone, Hallam,
Grote, Monckton Milnes joined him. A meeting
was held at the Freeman's Tavern to promote a
scheme for "a supply of good books in all departments of knowledge." Lord Eliot was in the chair,
and Carlyle made a fine speech. It is said to be his
only speech. Here are some sentences from it:

> A book is a kind of thing which requires a
> man to be self-collected. He must be alone
> with it. A good book is the purest essence
> of the human soul... The good of a book is
> not the facts that can be got out of it, but
> the kind of resonance that it awakes in our
> own minds. A book may strike out a thou-
> sand things, may make us know a thousand
> things which it does not know itself... The

founding of a Library is one of the greatest things we can do with regard to results. It is one of the quietest of things; but there is nothing that I know of at bottom more important. Everyone able to read a good book becomes a wiser man. He becomes a similar centre of light and order, and just insight into the things around him. A collection of good books contains all the nobleness and wisdom of the world before us. Every heroic and victorious soul has left his stamp upon it. A collection of books is the best of all Universities; for the University only teaches us to read the book: you must go to the book itself for what it is. I call it a Church also—which every devout soul may enter—a Church but with no quarrelling, no Church-rates...

At this point, Carlyle was interrupted by laughter and cheers, and sat down good-temperedly. His speech is too optimistic, in view of our present information; also too subjective in its emphasis on the "resonance" from books; also too little aware of the power of concentration possessed by many readers, which enables them to-day to continue through an air-raid. But it is a noble utterance. It recalls us to the importance of seriousness, and to the preciousness and the destructibility of knowledge. Knowledge will perish if we do not stand up for it, and testify. It is never safe, never harvested. It has to be protected not only against the gangster but against a much more charming and seductive foe: the crowd. "I know what I like and I know what I want," says the crowd, "and I don't want all these shelves and shelves of books. Scrap them."

The Library started in two rooms at 49 Pall Mall, with five hundred members, and three thousand books. Conditions were Spartan; no ink or paper was provided, and for a time there was no clock. In 1845 it moved into St. James's Square, and now it has a membership of four thousand, and about four hundred and seventy thousand books, together with various luxuries, including a comfortable reading-room. Its rise is largely due to a great librarian, Sir Charles Hagberg Wright, who died last year. Hagberg Wright had a European connection, and a European outlook. He was free from the insularity which has such a numbing effect on the collecting of books, and it is largely thanks to him that one feels the library to be not English but civilised. For the moment it has one overwhelming problem before it: that of not getting smashed and not getting burnt. But if normality returns it will have the task of getting into touch with the thought and literature of the Continent, however repellent the mental state of the Continent may be. And—a more congenial task—it will have to get up to date on America. It has never admitted, and it must never admit, the idea of exclusion; in Hagberg Wright's wise little pamphlet, *The Soul's Dispensary*, there are some pertinent remarks on this, and a curious account of the war which he had to wage after the last war with various government departments before he could regain liberty for the reimportation of foreign literature.

PUSHKIN PRESS—THE LONDON LIBRARY

"FOUND ON THE SHELVES"

THE LONDON LIBRARY (a registered charity) is one of the UK's leading literary institutions and a favourite haunt of authors, researchers and keen readers.

Membership is open to all.

Join at www.londonlibrary.co.uk.

www.pushkinpress.com